THE SEARCH

FOR A NEW BEGINNING:

Developing a New Civilization

by Mikhail Gorbachev

THE SEARCH

FOR A NEW BEGINNING:

Developing a New Civilization

by Mikhail Gorbachev

Translated by Pavel Palazchenko

HarperSanFrancisco
An Imprint of HarperCollins*Publishers*

Produced and Edited by: The Gorbachev Foundation
Book Design by: Frank Harrison Perez
State of the World Forum Logo by: Addison, Seefeld and Brew

FIRST EDITION

Library of Congress Cataloging-in-Publication Data
Gorbachev, Mikhail Sergeevich, 1931–
The search for a new beginning : developing a new civilization /
by Mikhail Gorbachev. — 1st ed.
p.   cm.
ISBN 0–06–251338–9
I. World politics—1898– I. Title.
D860.G665 1995   95-6443
909.82—dc20   CIP

95 96 97 98 99 ❖ HAD 10 9 8 7 6 5 4 3 2 1

CONTENTS

I.

THE SEARCH FOR

A NEW BEGINNING

. . . it is my firm belief that the infinite and uncontrollable fury of nuclear weapons should never be held in the hands of any mere mortal ever again, for any reason.

We are standing at the threshold of a new era on the frontier of two centuries and two millennia. Wherever we live, we all feel that we are at some kind of watershed and that we must change a great deal, both within our own countries and in relations between nations.

The present civilization, based on the imperatives of industrialism, the uncontrolled exploitation of human and natural resources, the social and national disintegration of people, social communities, nations, and states, and the restriction and suppression of human liberties, has exhausted itself. It is experiencing a serious crisis, in the course of which are arising new ways of living and the coexistence of peoples and states.

In the major centers of world politics the choice has been made in favor of peace, cooperation, interaction, and common security. In pushing forward to a new civilization we should under no circumstances make the error of interpreting victory in the "Cold War" narrowly as a victory for oneself, for one's own way of life, for one's own values and merits. This was a victory over a scheme for the development of humanity that was becoming slowly congealed and leading us to destruction. It was a shattering of the vicious circle into which we had driven ourselves. This was altogether a victory for common sense, reason, democracy, and common human values.

The world in which we live today is radically different from what it was at the beginning or even in the middle of this century. Our world continues to change, as do all its components. The advent of nuclear weapons was a tragic reminder of the fundamental nature of that change. A material symbol and expression of absolute military power, nuclear weapons at the same time revealed the absolute limits of that power.

Even if it now seems that the danger of nuclear annihilation presented by the Cold War is over and mercifully behind us, it is my firm belief that the infinite and uncontrollable fury of nuclear weapons should never be held in the hands of any mere mortal ever again, for any reason.

There is great peril in allowing ourselves to be lulled by a soothing but incorrect sense that because the Cold War has ended, the nuclear danger has eased and no longer requires urgent attention. If anything, this false sense of security makes the mortal danger that yet lurks in the shadow of our unfolding new affairs more perilous than ever.

The danger that has become apparent is what I would call the new arms race. I am referring to the continuing global proliferation of the most dangerous kinds of military technologies and the real threat of the spread of nuclear and other weapons of mass destruction. Furthermore, the advanced countries are turning out increasingly sophisticated weapons, and many conventional arms are assuming the quality of "absolute weapons."

In the final analysis, the nuclear threat is a direct product of the cult of force that has dominated the world for centuries. It is, if you will, its supreme incarnation. For it is more than just someone's threat to use force against another. It stands for the readiness to physically destroy the adversary. It is a kind of mental illness, the loss of reason that *Homo sapiens* must possess. The world of interdependence and cooperation must absolutely rule out the use of force, particularly of nuclear weapons, as the solution to any problems.

The world must take a series of interrelated and properly timed steps to alleviate further the nuclear danger. These should include further deep cuts in the Russian and American nuclear arsenals, with the other nuclear powers joining the process; the cessation of the production of weapons-grade plutonium; the complete and final cessation of nuclear weapons testing without exception; strengthening the International Atomic Energy Agency, extending its jurisdiction to the supplies of all "near nuclear" materials; and the substantial extension and modification of the Nuclear Non-Proliferation Treaty.

I am committed to a nuclear-free world. Whereas I understand those who are mindful of possible aggressive ambitions of some rogue dictator or authoritarian regime, *I believe that a new structure of international relations, which I here propose, combined with the absolute superiority of democratic nations in sophisticated conventional arms, provide guarantees that are quite sufficient for genuine national security in the new world order.*

II.

THE ROOTS OF THE

CURRENT CRISIS

The twentieth century must be seen as a century of warning, a call of caution to humankind . . .

The twentieth century must be seen as a *century of warning,* a call of caution to humankind for the necessity of developing a new consciousness and new ways of living and acting. Has it fulfilled this role? No, at least not completely.

It has been the fond hope of many that the end of the Cold War would liberate the international community to work together to avert threats and work in a spirit of cooperation in addressing the dangerous problems that affect the world as a whole. But, despite the numerous summit meetings, conferences, congresses, negotiations, and agreements, there does not appear to have been any tangible progress.

In all likelihood, no one—neither the political leaders nor any other thinking individual—really believed that right after the end of the Cold War we would immediately start living under a new world order. *Between the old order and the new one lies a period of transition that we must go through*—moving toward a new structure of international relations marked by cooperating, interacting, and taking advantage of new opportunities.

What we are actually seeing today, however, looks rather like a world disorder.

It is my belief that today's policy makers lack a necessary sense of perspective and the ability to evaluate the consequences of their actions. What is absolutely necessary is a critical reassessment of the views and approaches that currently lie at the basis of political thinking and a new combination of players to envision and carry us through to the next phase of human development.

The world is truly at a crossroads. We face many complex problems whose solutions will take more than just physical resources and financial expenditures. To meet these challenges the rules of international behavior will have to be changed. The roots of the current crisis of civilization lie within humanity itself. Our intellectual and moral development is lagging behind the rapidly changing conditions of our existence, and we are finding it difficult to adjust psychologically to the pace of change. *Only by renouncing selfishness and attempts to out-*

smart one another to gain an advantage at the expense of others can we hope to ensure the survival of humankind and the further development of our civilization.

Each generation inherits from its predecessors the material and spiritual wealth of civilization. And each generation is responsible for preserving this inheritance and developing it for the succeeding generations.

Human beings do not choose the times in which they live. It has fallen to our lot to live in extremely dramatic times.

Ours is a time of acute problems and unprecedented opportunities. We shall be able to accomplish our historic task of developing our inheritance only if, irrespective of our political opinions, religious beliefs, or philosophies, we try to understand and help one another and act in concert for a better future.

III.

THE CHALLENGES

WE FACE

. . . the international community is now confronted with problems that we are only now beginning to understand.

A unique feature of this time of transition is that the civilization that came into being several centuries ago has now brought us to a point when *humankind has become mortal.* We have suddenly become like careless children whose vigor and activity far exceed the development of their morality and consciousness.

True, we have found in ourselves the courage to put an end to one of the threats to our existence—the threat of a global nuclear war. At least, its main source—the Cold War—has been abolished.

But, having consigned this threat to the past, the international community is now confronted with problems that we are only now beginning to understand. These include:

• Increased nationalism, separatism, and the process of disintegration in a number of countries.

• The growing gap in the level and quality of socioeconomic development between rich and poor countries. Only one-third of humanity has good food, good hygiene, and good health care. The rest suffer from hunger and die at an early age. The wealth of some means the poverty of others. Through television, those in poverty can see the material well-being of the wealthy. Hence the unprecedented passions and brutality and even fanaticism of mass protests. Here, too, is the breeding ground for the spread of terrorism and the emergence and persistence of dictatorial regimes with their unpredictable behavior in relations among states.

• The fueling of a destructive development that has brought the planet to the edge of a great ecological crisis simply in order to maintain the living standard of those who are privileged by history and circumstances. The environmental dangers that threaten all of us are not one hundred or two hundred years away. They could strike us down within the next two or three decades, the span of a single generation.

• The gap between basically peaceful policies and selfish economies bent on achieving a kind of technological hegemony. Unless these two vectors are brought together, civilization will tend to break down into incompatible sectors.

• Further improvement in modern weaponry, even if under the pretext of strengthening security. This may result not only in a new spiral of the arms race and a perilous overabundance of arms in many states, but also in a final divorce between the process of disarmament and development, and, what is more, in an erosion of the foundations and criteria of the emerging new world politics.

Timely solutions are not being found to these enormous planetary problems not only because we have been too slow to realize their gravity and danger. The main reason is that these global problems require joint action on a worldwide scale—but the Cold War impeded such action. It is only now that we recognize the real menace that these problems represent. *The end of the Cold War has also brought to the fore tensions that were latent, frozen as it were, during the confrontation between the global alliances.* Many of these tensions have exploded into bloody conflicts.

Thus, two sets of problems have emerged, some of *global* dimensions, such as the environment, world economy, populations, energy, food, and health, and some of *political* dimensions, both international and national in scope. They are interrelated and interdependent. This is a sign of our times, which testifies to the real rather than imaginary integral wholeness of the world, something that dictates its own laws and ground rules. For this whole is more than the sum of its components—it requires a new quality of existence.

The time has come to develop integrated global policies. This need is all the greater since the obvious crisis of the entire system of international relations is just one of the manifestations of the malaise of our civilization.

The future is challenging us. But humanity is capable of meeting the challenge. *We will meet the challenge if we become aware of the world's unity, of humankind's common destiny,* and of the responsibility of every one of us for the preservation of life on Earth.

IV.

THE GREENING

OF POLITICS

. . . humanity's disregard for the environment presents the greatest threat to our immediate future.

If nuclear weapons constituted the greatest threat to our immediate past, humanity's disregard for the environment presents the greatest threat to our immediate future. Concern for the environment brings together the consequences of various destructive processes—from uncontrolled development of technologies that destroy nature, including humankind, to the population explosions; from unbridled consumerism to the ever-widening gap in the living standards of various countries and regions.

Even today, nature is meting out severe punishment for our arrogant disregard of its existence, laws, and needs. In the face of this, humanity must consciously change its relations with the rest of nature. The idea that the present generations inherited from the Age of Enlightenment, that "humanity is the king of nature," is the psychological and spiritual prerequisite of the current environmental crisis. *We need a new paradigm that will bring us back to reality, recognizing that humanity is just a part of nature,* that our own future, our destiny as well as that of our planet, depends on our attitude to the world around us.

The time has come for humankind to accept the traditional philosophy of the Native Americans: We do not inherit this planet from our parents, we are borrowing it from our children.

Humanity is part of the biosphere, is one with the biosphere.

We must not forget that clean water, oxygen in the air, and soil productivity are the result of the interaction of hundreds of thousands of plant, animal, and microorganic species, the components of the ecosystem. The durability of ecosystems and, consequently, the quality of the environment, depends on preserving and maintaining biological diversity and the balance of the biosphere.

The greening of politics is a new view of the problem of consumption and its rationalization. The raising of people's living standards must not be done at the cost of exhausting nature. It should be accompanied by the conservation and renewal of the living conditions of the plant and animal world.

The greening of politics also affects approaches to tackling many social problems connected primarily with damage to people's health as a result of the harm already done to the environment.

The greening of politics means maximum support for scientific research and fundamental disciplines that study the biosphere and its ecosystem.

The greening of politics is an affirmation of the priority of values common to humanity, enriching education and upbringing with ecological content from childhood onward and developing a new and modern attitude toward nature. At the same time, *the greening of politics is the return to humankind of the awareness of humanity as a part of nature.* The moral improvement of society and the maturation of civilization is inconceivable without this.

V.

COMMON LESSONS OF

THE PAST

. . . artificially constructed utopian schemes are not workable anywhere . . .

The recognition of the world as an *integral whole* calls for a change in our value system, or to put it more precisely, for actualizing the initial values that are inherent in the nature of the human being as a social and spiritual entity. In one form or another, and in varying degrees, those values are reflected in the world religions and in the great humanistic doctrines.

Politicians and ideologues perverted them by making them instruments of evil. But the time has come when those values, in their modern interpretation, are becoming indispensable for the survival and betterment of humankind.

All of us should draw lessons from both the recent and the distant past. For centuries, history was a chaotic process that evolved as a result of individual and group actions, despite all attempts to make it more orderly and channel it along reasonable lines. The world was groping for a way forward. Whether consciously or not, it followed the famous maxim, "They who persevere will travel the road." But in our time this chaotic process has unleashed tremendous forces of both a constructive and a destructive nature. No longer can we afford to act in this manner. *We need a clear vision of where we are, whence we are moving, and what we want to achieve.* Our slogan should be, "They who see far ahead will travel the road."

Conflicts and wars have been an organic part of history. Now the time has come to think about the victims of our many tragic delusions, from the Crusades to the Cold War. One of the paradoxes of the twentieth century is the inconsistency between the enormous technological achievements of humankind and the often pitiable situation in our spiritual and moral development. How else can we explain the fact that in the twentieth century whole nations became victims to genocide? The Holocaust of World War II was one of the most terrible crimes of Nazism. *The Holocaust should be a reminder about the dangers in democracy,* about the imperfections of the existing democratic systems, and about the special responsibility of all those who are committed to democracy, not just in words, but in deeds.

I am convinced that we all can learn common lessons from both the recent and the more remote past. One such lesson from history is that artificially constructed utopian schemes are not workable anywhere — either in Eastern or Western Europe, or on any continent. From our own experience, we know that such approaches are flawed and inherently unworkable. I think that the strategy for the future should be grounded in existing realities, based on a thorough and entirely pragmatic analysis of their potential development. The next lesson, in my view, is to renounce drastic, revolutionary breaks. The idea of leaping ahead of one's time is tempting, but the consequences of such "leaps forward" are very dangerous. Hence, while responding to the requirements of our time and keeping pace with them, we must move forward in an evolutionary way, step by step, identifying the emerging problems. *Learning the lessons of the past means rejecting any kind of intolerance, impatience, and maximalism, persisting in a search for common interests,* and avoiding relapses, particularly hasty recourse to the use of force.

Finally, I think we all must understand that democracy is something more than just a political principle or the elections of parliaments or presidents. Democracy means moral values, without which democracy can deteriorate and degenerate, often leading to the establishment of authoritarian and totalitarian regimes. Democracy means stable political institutions, based on the primacy of law and justice, and rooted in the traditions of nations and in public consciousness. Democracy is not guaranteed against defeat. Democracy will always be tested. Democracy has many overt and covert clothes and many false friends. *Democracy does not come by itself. It must always be nurtured and protected.*

VI.

THE NEED

FOR NEW POLITICS

. . . all members of the world community should resolutely discard old stereotypes and motivations nurtured by the Cold War . . .

On the eve of the twenty-first century, the world needs new politics. But even though that seems indisputable, it can only become a reality if and when government leaders, however preoccupied with their countries' day-to-day problems, begin aligning their actions with the global challenges that face humankind.

I know this from my own experience. In domestic politics, we responded to the new challenges of the Soviet Union in the 1980s with the policies of *perestroika* and *glasnost*. These policies impelled the development of democracy and the movement toward freedom. Our quest for a new foreign policy was based on the philosophy of "new thinking." Many of the world community's leading players responded to it. Its principal result was the ending of the Cold War.

Risking something new, we did not always succeed. In the early years of *perestroika*, we formulated the principle "Start *perestroika* with yourself." In fact, however, we rushed to change society while leaving the change of ourselves for later times. That was the root cause of many of our mistakes, miscalculations, and failures. And it is even more true of today's Russia, in which the growing discrepancy between the spontaneous process of change and conscious efforts at self-improvement has had unfortunate consequences.

Nevertheless, *perestroika* and *glasnost* changed Russia and the world. International relations now have to be conducted in a new framework. This does not mean that things have become easier. We are facing new, extremely complex problems and unexpected difficulties.

I am convinced that in order to solve these problems *there is no other way but to seek and implement new forms of interaction.* We must simply find such new interactions — otherwise we shall be unable to consolidate positive trends that have emerged and are gaining strength, and that opportunity simply must not be sacrificed.

In this regard, I would like to emphasize three points:

• First, today more than ever before there is a need to join politics with morality. In a world oversaturated with dangers, every step and every action of states, and not just states but public organizations, movements, and parties, must be highly responsible.

• The second point, another requirement of our time, is unqualified compliance with international law. Today, international law is a product of the collective efforts of virtually all states that comprise the United Nations. What they create together must be put into effect with unswerving determination.

• Finally, the third element is fairness and justice. It would be an illusion to believe that at the present stage of social development it is possible to guarantee the satisfaction of everyone's essential needs. But, even now, we can and must ensure that international disputes be settled on the basis of justice and law; that the strong help the weak rise to their feet, rather than hold them down; that those who deliberately violate treaties and obligations be punished without fail.

To accomplish these goals, all members of the world community should resolutely discard old stereotypes and motivations nurtured by the Cold War, and give up the habit of seeking one another's weak points and exploiting them in their own interests. Even if human rights and freedoms are observed throughout the world under democracies, peculiarities and differences will always exist. We must respect these differences. With the end of confrontation, differences can be made a source of healthy competition, an important factor for progress. This is an incentive to study one another, to engage in exchanges, a prerequisite for the growth of mutual trust.

VII.

A CALL

FOR NEW VALUES

It is time for every individual, nation, and state to rethink its place and role in world affairs.

One of the paradoxes of the twentieth century is the gap between humankind's amazing technological achievements and the often deplorable state of the human spirit and human morality. We saw the collapse of the attempt that was made in Soviet Russia and other countries to construct a "new system of values" and to impose on people norms of behavior that were said to reflect their true interest. In reality, this attempt "to make humankind happy" resulted in something totally unacceptable to the civilized world: namely, humanity's alienation from property and power, making the individual a "cog in the wheel" of a thoroughly ideologized machinery of the state.

On the other hand, it is increasingly evident that the values of the Western world are becoming more and more anachronistic. Their Golden Age is in the past; neither can assure a dependable future for the human race.

We should take a sober and unprejudiced view of the strengths and weaknesses of collectivism, which is fraught with the problems inherent in dictatorship. But what about the individualism of Western culture? At the very least, something must be done about its purely consumerist orientation that emphasizes "having" rather than "being," acquiring and possessing rather than revealing the real potential of humanity.

Today, humankind is facing a choice. It is time for every individual, nation, and state to rethink its place and role in world affairs. We need an intellectual breakthrough into a new dimension. And that means that the state of the human spirit assumes paramount importance. The roles of culture, religion, science, and education must grow enormously. The responsibility of the centers of humanity's intellectual, scientific, and religious development is immense and must be given preeminence.

The future of human society will not be defined in terms of capitalism versus socialism. It was that dichotomy that caused the division of the world community into two blocs and brought about so many catastrophic consequences. *We need to find a paradigm that will integrate all the achievements of the human mind and human action, irrespective of which ideology or political movement can be credited with them.* This paradigm can only be based on the common values that humankind has developed over many centuries. The search for a new paradigm should be a search for synthesis, for what is common to and unites people, countries, and nations, rather than what divides them.

The search for such a synthesis can succeed if the following conditions are met.

•   First of all, we must return to the well-known human values that are embodied in the ideals of the world religions and also in the socialist ideas that inherited much from those values.

•   Further, we need to search for a new paradigm of development that is based on those values and that is capable of leading us all toward a genuinely humanistic or, more precisely, humanistic-ecological culture of living.

•   Finally, we need to develop methods of social action and policy that will direct society to a path consistent with the interests of both humanity and the rest of nature.

When I speak of a new synthesis, of the need for increasing unity and interdependence, I am not calling for a kind of universal leveling, sameness, or uniformity. I do not accept a civilization that would be like a huge historic steamroller, flattening out everything. Who would need such a new civilization, and why even call it new? By no means do I want all countries and nations to become alike. *I think that the civilization to which we all belong is one of great multiplicity. And that is a source of its strength,* the basis for the exchange of cultural values, for comparing methods of organization and ways of living.

The philosophy of the twenty-first century must be grounded in a philosophy of diversity. If life as such is the highest value, then even more precious is the singular identity of every nation and every race as a unique creation of nature and human history.

At the same time, we must begin to define certain moral maxims or ethical commandments that constitute values common to all humankind. It is my view that the individual's attitude toward nature must become one of the principal criteria for ensuring the maintenance of morality. Today it is not enough to say, "Thou shalt not kill." Ecological education implies, above all, respect and love for every living being. It is here that ecological culture interfaces with religion.

The beauty and uniqueness of life lies in the unity of diversity. Self-identification—of every individual and of the many different nations, ethnic groups, and nationalities—is the crucial condition for preserving life on Earth. Struggles and conflicts burn out the diversity of life, leaving a social wasteland in their wake. Honoring diversity and honoring the earth creates the basis for genuine unity.

VIII.

DEVELOPING A NEW

CIVILIZATION

*In the final analysis the main source of our
troubles is not outside, but within us . . .*

We face the task of developing a new civilization. New in that its evolution should be consistent with the new conditions of humankind's existence. New in that it should abolish the confrontational spirit and thinking that underpinned all past civilizations and are still present today. New in that this civilization must be a civilization of all humankind, responding realistically and constructively to the challenge of interdependence.

The whole world is at the threshold of dramatic changes. Moreover, this will not be just one more transition from one stage to another, of which there have been so many in history. Many signs indicate that it will be a watershed of historic scope and significance, with a new civilization coming to replace the existing one.

The time has come to choose a new direction of global development, to opt for a new civilization. Today we can only chart its most general outlines. It is a civilization that rules out confrontational approaches. Economic, political, class, interethnic, or ideological wars will have to be abolished. The use of force as a political tool will have to be rejected. Cooperation will gradually supplant competition. It will be a civilization of mutual tolerance, with cultures and nations becoming increasingly open-minded and diversity understood and used as a factor of progress. And, first and foremost, it will be a civilization that assures harmony and creative coexistence between humanity and the rest of nature.

To build this new civilization, a higher level of responsibility and mutual trust is required among individuals embracing the new order of things. Senior statespeople, current political and spiritual leaders, business executives, scientists, artists, youth, and intellectuals must improve their interaction at both national and international levels.

The statespeople who ended the Cold War established for the first time in modern history the possibility of a truly global peace. In new ways, therefore, our current political leaders are challenged to provide the framework for stability and regulated human interactions; our moral leaders to give expression to the eternal values that have always guided humanity; the business community to assume responsibility for the investment and innovation necessary for prosperity; scientists to take into consideration the ethical and environmental implications of their technological developments; artists to express metaphorically our dreams and tragedies; our youth to demand that the future be better than the past; and intellectuals to offer penetrating insight concerning humanity's progress toward shared goals. *Only the creative interaction of these groups, rather than the supremacy of one group over the others, will allow the answers we all seek to emerge* and guide us as we shape the next phase of human development.

The fact that it is possible to bring such diverse aspects of the human community together, not only in principle but in practice, has been demonstrated recently in the very areas in which trust and cooperation were regarded as unthinkable just a few years before.

There is simply no other way to cope with the current "world disorder" and rampant chaos. The crisis of modern civilization has caused tremendous damage to humankind. It is undermining social ties, family life, moral principles, and values. Many people are acting irresponsibly, as though they followed the iniquitous old maxim, "After us, the deluge." The evil of this kind of philosophy and behavior is that it propels humankind toward self-destruction.

In the final analysis the main source of our troubles is not outside, but within us, in our attitudes toward one another, toward society and nature. All the rest derives from that. We therefore must first change ourselves, through self-education and multidisciplinary, world-wide, and cross-generational interaction. And, having changed ourselves, we must come together in all our diversity to build a new world.

IX.

THE NEXT FRONTIER

. . . it is the personal involvement of each and every individual that will allow a new civilization to flourish on Earth.

My most urgent message is that *it is time for every person and every nation to rethink their role in global development.* Everyone needs to be involved. Everyone has a role to play.

Our political leaders need new overall guidelines. World science alone is not capable of developing them. It is the bringing together of politics, science, religion, and morality that will provide the key to solving the problems that humankind is facing today. And it is the personal involvement of each and every individual that will allow a new civilization to flourish on Earth.

Time and time again I go back to the words of John Kennedy: "We stand today on the edge of a new frontier—a frontier of unknown opportunities and perils, a frontier of unfulfilled hopes and threats." Today, almost thirty years later, we are even more acutely aware that it would be criminal to miss the chance to carry through the historic shifts that have been maturing for so long, and that we vitally need a policy worthy of the scientific and technical achievements of the times and of the new discoveries promised in the century to come.

It is very close, and many of us will live to witness its onset. They say that humanity is always seized by anxiety at the turn of a millennium. Today there is reason for that. The end of the Cold War, the emancipation of my country and of Eastern Europe, has inspired all of us. But the manifestations of chaos, collapse, and loss of control demand that we bend every effort to seek the paths to an intelligent and necessarily democratic organization of our common abode.

I have no ready-made solutions. I do not believe in imposing models and schemes on society. I believe in the individual, in the potential of intellect and conscience. Like the great American writer William Faulkner, I refuse to accept the end of humankind, however severe our future trials may be.

STATE
of the
WORLD
FORUM